Date: 2/3/12

Home on the Earth

A Song About Earth's Layers

by Laura Purdie Salas

illustrated by Viviana Garofoli

Sing along to the tune of

"Home on the Range."

Learn about the matter that makes up our planet.

PICTURE WINDOW BOOKS

Minneapolis, Minnesota

Editor: Jill Kalz
Designer: Abbey Fitzgerald
Page Production: Melissa Kes
Art Director: Nathan Gassman
Editorial Director: Nick Healy
The illustrations in this book were created digitally.

Picture Window Books
151 Good Counsel Drive, P.O. Box 669
Mankato, MN 56002-0669
877-845-8392
www.picturewindowbooks.com

Printed in the United States of America.

 All books published by Picture Window Books
are manufactured with paper containing at least
10 percent post-consumer waste.

Library of Congress Cataloging-in-Publication Data
Salas, Laura Purdie.
Home on the Earth : a song about Earth's layers / by Laura Purdie Salas ;
illustrated by Viviana Garofoli.
p. cm. – (Science Songs)
Includes index.
ISBN 978-1-4048-5296-9 (library binding)
1. Earth sciences–Juvenile literature 2. Earth–Juvenile literature. 3. Earth sciences–
Songs and music. 4. Science–Songs and music. I. Garofoli, Viviana ill. II. Title.
QE29.S26 2009
550–dc22
2008038429

Thanks to our advisers for their expertise, research, and advice:

Virg Debban, Secondary Science Teacher (ret.)
New Ulm (Minnesota) Public School ISD #88

Terry Flaherty, Ph.D., Professor of English
Minnesota State University, Mankato

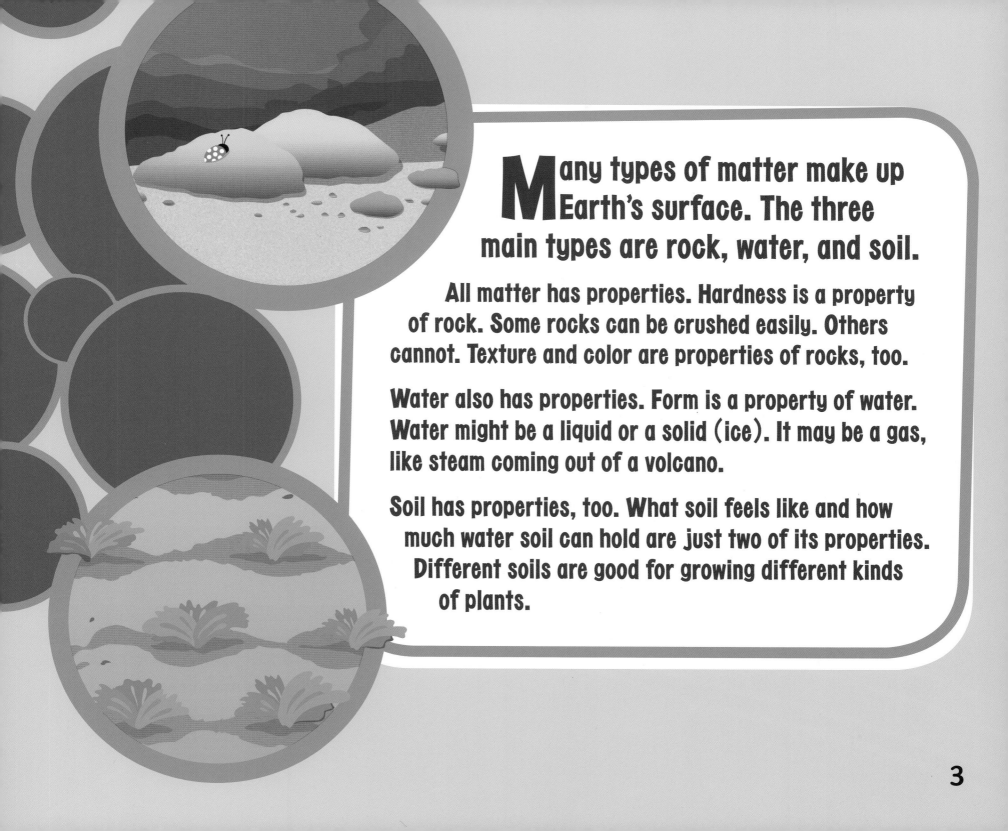

Many types of matter make up Earth's surface. The three main types are rock, water, and soil.

All matter has properties. Hardness is a property of rock. Some rocks can be crushed easily. Others cannot. Texture and color are properties of rocks, too.

Water also has properties. Form is a property of water. Water might be a liquid or a solid (ice). It may be a gas, like steam coming out of a volcano.

Soil has properties, too. What soil feels like and how much water soil can hold are just two of its properties. Different soils are good for growing different kinds of plants.

Go take a short walk, look around at some rock,

See the mountains and cliff sides so tall.

4

Rocks are made of different minerals. Graphite is one example of a mineral. It is used in pencil lead.

They wear down and break, and eventually make

Many pebbles and sand grains so small.

7

Home, home on the Earth,

With its gases to breathe all around,

Where the sun forms a breeze over deep-water seas,

And the soil and the rocks make the ground.

Soil is partly made of rocks and minerals that have broken down into tiny pieces. Dead plants and animals also form soil as they decay.

Don't ever forget that the ocean is wet;

It protects Earth from getting too dry.

We need water to drink; it's amazing to think

That it falls from the clouds in the sky.

Earth has a water cycle. Rain falls from clouds. It fills rivers. Rivers flow to the oceans. The sun heats up the ocean water. The water evaporates and makes clouds. Then the cycle starts all over again.

Home, home on the Earth,

With its gases to breathe all around,

Where the sun forms a breeze over deep-water seas,

And the soil and the rocks make the ground.

Earth's atmosphere includes the air we breathe. You cannot see, taste, or touch air. But when the wind blows, you can feel air move.

15

Oh, what can it be, this clear gas you can't see,

That we move through as if it's not there?

16

Well we can't live without what we're talking about;

It's the mixture that we all call air.

The air we breathe is called the atmosphere. Several gases make up the atmosphere. The biggest part of it is a gas called nitrogen. The gas called oxygen is only about one-fifth of Earth's atmosphere.

19

Home, home on the Earth,

With its gases to breathe all around,

Where the sun forms a breeze over deep-water seas,

And the soil and the rocks make the ground.

water

rock

Home on the Earth

(Verse)
Go take a short walk, look a-round at some rock, See the

moun- tains and cliff sides so tall. They wear down and break, and e-

ven- tu- ally make Many pe- bbles and sand grains so small.

(Chorus)
Home, home on the Earth, With its ga- ses to

breathe all a- round, Where the sun forms a breeze o- ver

deep- wa- ter seas, And the soil and the rocks make the ground.

2. Don't ever forget that the ocean is wet;
It protects Earth from getting too dry.
We need water to drink; it's amazing to think
That it falls from the clouds in the sky.

3. Oh, what can it be, this clear gas you can't see,
That we move through as if it's not there?
Well we can't live without what we're
talking about;
It's the mixture that we all call air.

The audio file for this book is available
for download at:
http://www.capstonekids.com/sciencesongs.html

22

air

Did You Know?

Earth's crust is made of rock. But the crust is not one solid piece. It is made of about a dozen huge pieces and many little pieces.

Over time, rain, snow, wind, ocean waves, and even the warmth of the sun help wear down big rocks into small pebbles and sand.

The world has five oceans with names: Arctic, Atlantic, Indian, Pacific, and Southern. But they are all connected. So there is really only one ocean. It covers more than half of Earth's surface.

Fossils are the remains of plants and animals that lived long ago. Scientists study fossils to learn about Earth's past.

Glossary

atmosphere—the gases that surround a planet

decay—to break down into tiny pieces after dying

evaporate—to change from a liquid to a gas

matter—what things are made of; materials

minerals—types of rocks; copper and iron are two minerals

property—something that is true about all examples of one thing

texture—the way something feels

To Learn More

More Books to Read

Green, Jen. *Rocks and Soil.* New York: PowerKids Press, 2008.

Mayer, Cassie. *Oceans and Seas.* Chicago: Heinemann Library, 2008.

Rosinsky, Natalie. *Dirt: The Scoop on Soil.* Minneapolis: Picture Window Books, 2003.

Stewart, Melissa. *Air Is Everywhere.* Minneapolis: Compass Point Books, 2005.

Index

On the Web

FactHound offers a safe, fun way to find educator-approved Internet sites related to this book.

Here's what you do:

1. Visit *www.facthound.com*
2. Choose your grade level.
3. Begin your search.

This book's ID number is 9781404852969

Look for all of the books in the Science Songs series:

♪ Are You Living?
A Song About Living and Nonliving Things

♪ From Beginning to End:
A Song About Life Cycles

♪ Home on the Earth:
A Song About Earth's Layers

♪ Move It! Work It!
A Song About Simple Machines